D1295220

DEC   2017

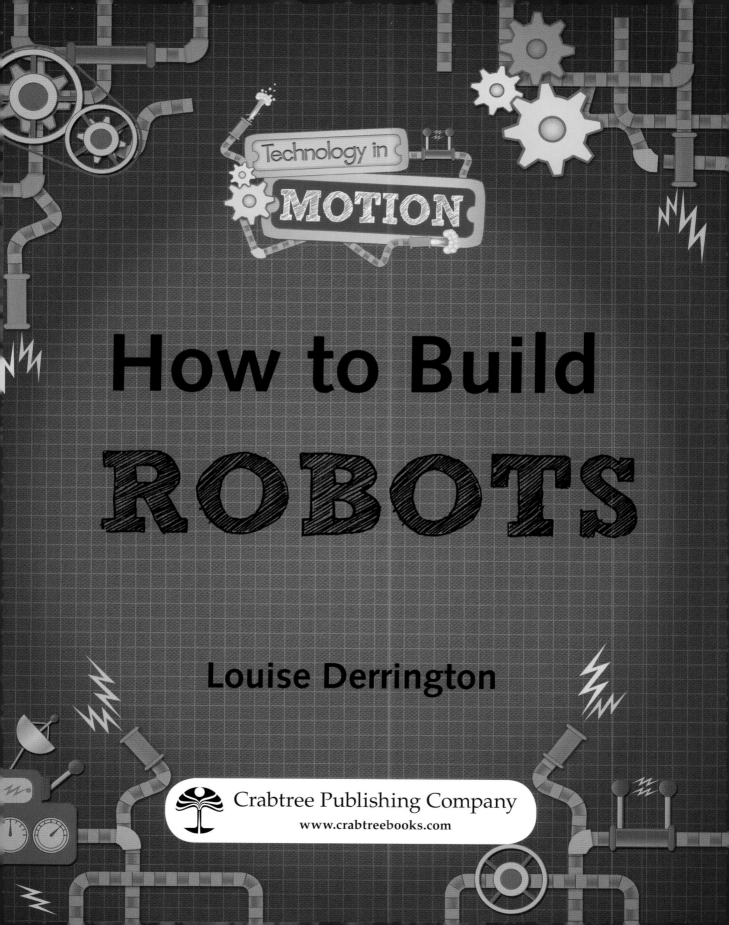

Technology in MOTION

How to Build
ROBOTS

Louise Derrington

Crabtree Publishing Company
www.crabtreebooks.com

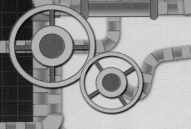

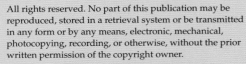

Technology in MOTION

Crabtree Publishing Company
www.crabtreebooks.com
1-800-387-7650

Published in Canada
Crabtree Publishing
616 Welland Avenue
St. Catharines, ON
L2M 5V6

Published in the United States
Crabtree Publishing
PMB 59051
350 Fifth Ave, 59th Floor
New York, NY 10118

Published in 2017 by CRABTREE PUBLISHING COMPANY.

First published in 2016 by The Watts Publishing Group (A division of Hachette Children's Books)
Copyright © The Watts Publishing Group 2016

Author: Louise Derrington

Editorial director: Adrian Cole

Project Coordinator: Kathy Middleton

Editors: Petrice Custance

Designer manager: Peter Scoulding

Cover design and illustrations: Cathryn Gilbert

Proofreader: Wendy Scavuzzo

Prepress technician: Samara Parent

Print and production coordinator: Katherine Berti

The publisher would like to thank the following for their kind permission to reproduce their photographs:

The publishers would like to thank the following for permission to reproduce their photos: Deymos.HR / Shutterstock.com: 15; D J Shin: 29 (top); Greg Mitchell – United States Navy: 4 (bottom); Guzugi at English Wikipedia: 29 (bottom); Jon Ray: 5 (top); NASA: 5 (middle); Xavier Caré / Wikimedia Commons / CC-BY-SA: 5: (bottom); Zen wave: 4 (top).

Step-by-step photography by Tudor Photography, Banbury.

Every attempt has been made to clear copyright. Should there be any inadvertent omission, please apply to the publisher for rectification.

The website addresses (URLs) included in this book were valid at the time of going to press. However, it is possible that contents or addresses may have changed since the publication of this book. No responsibility for any such changes can be accepted by either the author or the Publisher.

Printed in Hong Kong/012017/BK20171024

Library and Archives Canada Cataloguing in Publication

Derrington, Louise, author
   How to build robots / Louise Derrington.

(Technology in motion)
Issued in print and electronic formats.
ISBN 978-0-7787-3394-2 (hardback).--
ISBN 978-0-7787-3397-3 (paperback).--
ISBN 978-1-4271-1908-7 (html)

   1. Robotics--Juvenile literature. 2. Robots--Juvenile literature.I. Title.

TJ211.2.D47 2016   j629.8'92   C2016-906631-2
                                    C2016-906632-0

Library of Congress Cataloging-in-Publication Data

Names: Derrington, Louise, author.
Title: How to build robots / Louise Derrington.
Description: New York, NY : Crabtree Publishing Company, 2017.
   Series: Technology in motion | "First published in 2016 by The Watts Publishing Group." | Includes index.
Identifiers: LCCN 2016045925 (print) | LCCN 2016049738 (ebook)
   ISBN 9780778733942 (hardcover) |
   ISBN 9780778733973 (pbk.) |
   ISBN 9781427119087 (Electronic book text)
Subjects: LCSH: Robots--Design and construction--Juvenile literature. | Robotics--Juvenile literature.
Classification: LCC TJ211.2 .D47 2017 (print) | LCC TJ211.2 (ebook) | DDC 629.8/92--dc23
LC record available at https://lccn.loc.gov/2016045925

Contents

SAFETY FIRST
Some of the projects in this book require scissors, sharp tools, and a hot glue gun. We recommend that children be supervised by a responsible adult for the undertaking of each project in this book.

What is a robot?

Robots are machines that are capable of carrying out a series of actions automatically. They perform complicated, useful, and sometimes dangerous jobs. They are intelligent machines but, unlike humans, they cannot think for themselves.

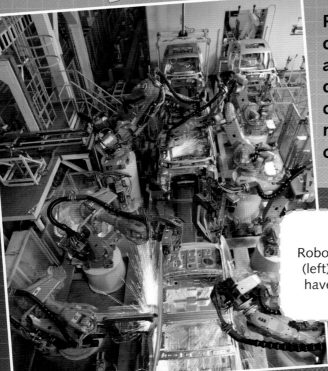

Robots in the workplace

Robots have changed the way we make things, from cars (left) to computers. Robots do not get bored when they have to do the same things over and over again, which makes them very efficient.

Robots in danger

Robots help us in some of the most dangerous places on Earth. They are used to detect and dispose of bombs. They can also be fitted with **sensors** and be sent into **contaminated** areas to collect information about levels of chemicals and **radiation**.

Robots in medicine

Robots are already used by doctors performing surgery. Researchers are investigating many more ways that robots could be useful, including the development of tiny robots which will be able to squeeze through the narrowest **blood vessels** to perform medical procedures.

The new generation of **prostheses**, or artificial limbs, are called **myoelectrics**. These robotic limbs are powered by electrical signals from the remaining muscles of the limb.

Robots in the home

As more and more people study robotics, they come up with inventive ideas for how robots can help us at home. Indoors, there are robot cleaners to wash floors and vacuum carpets. Outdoors, there are robots to mow the lawn and clean swimming pools. In Japan and elsewhere, research is underway to see whether robot pets can help elderly people by providing companionship.

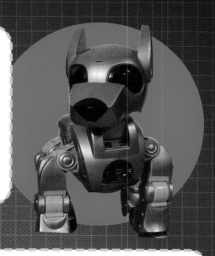

From the heights to the depths

Robotic arms (left) are used to perform tasks in space, as well as under the sea. Robotic arms have been used on the International Space Station to help with building work and repairs. **Autonomous** underwater vehicles (AUVs) are used to map the ocean bed.

robotic arm in use on the International Space Station

Artificial intelligence

Some robots have artificial intelligence, which means they are able to show some forms of human behavior. These robots can recognize faces, play games, and talk. Some of them even look like people and seem able to make decisions—but that isn't the case. Robots are only tools to help us get things done. Robots are still limited by the information they are given by humans.

Before you get started on each of the projects in this book, you'll need to gather together the materials and tools listed in the "you will need" box. Hopefully you will have most things on hand, but some of the more unusual items can be found at most hobby or electronics stores.

Basic robot hand

Make a robot hand that moves!

How does it work? When you pull the threads of your robot hand, the drinking straws close up and make the cardboard fingers curl. The drinking straws and threads of the robot hand mimic the action of the bones, **tendons**, **ligaments**, and muscles in a human hand.

To make a basic robot hand, you will need:
- pencil and thin white paper (for tracing the template)
- letter-sized sheet of thick paper
- scissors
- tube of clear all-purpose glue
- 5 drinking straws
- sticky tape
- 5 lengths of thick thread, 8 inches (20 cm) long

1 Use the template on page 30 to draw and cut out the hand with thick paper.

2 Make a line of glue down the center of each of the paper fingers and the thumb.

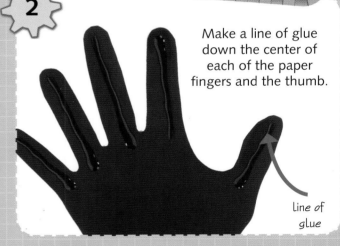

Line of glue

3 Cut 11 pieces of drinking straw (3 for each of the three middle fingers and 2 for the little finger). Place them on the lines of glue, leaving a 0.25-inch (6 mm) gap between each piece.

0.25-inch (6 mm) gap

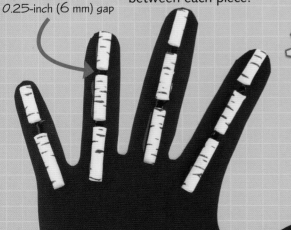

4 Cut two pieces of drinking straw so that they fit on the line of glue on the thumb, leaving a 0.25-inch (6 mm) gap between each piece. Attach them on the line of glue.

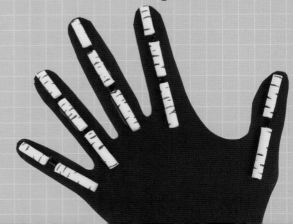

5 Make five more lines of glue, stretching between the bottom of each paper finger and the wrist. Cut the straws so that they line up at the wrist, leaving at least 0.25-inches (6 mm) below the straws on the fingers and thumb. Stick them on the lines of glue. Leave to dry.

0.25-inch (6 mm) gap

6 Turn the paper hand over. Use sticky tape to tape a length of thick thread to the top of each finger and the thumb.

7 Turn the paper hand over again. Bring each thread from the back over the end of each finger and down through the pieces of drinking straw. Gather all five threads and tie them together.

8 Pull the strings. The fingers will bend toward you along the joints.

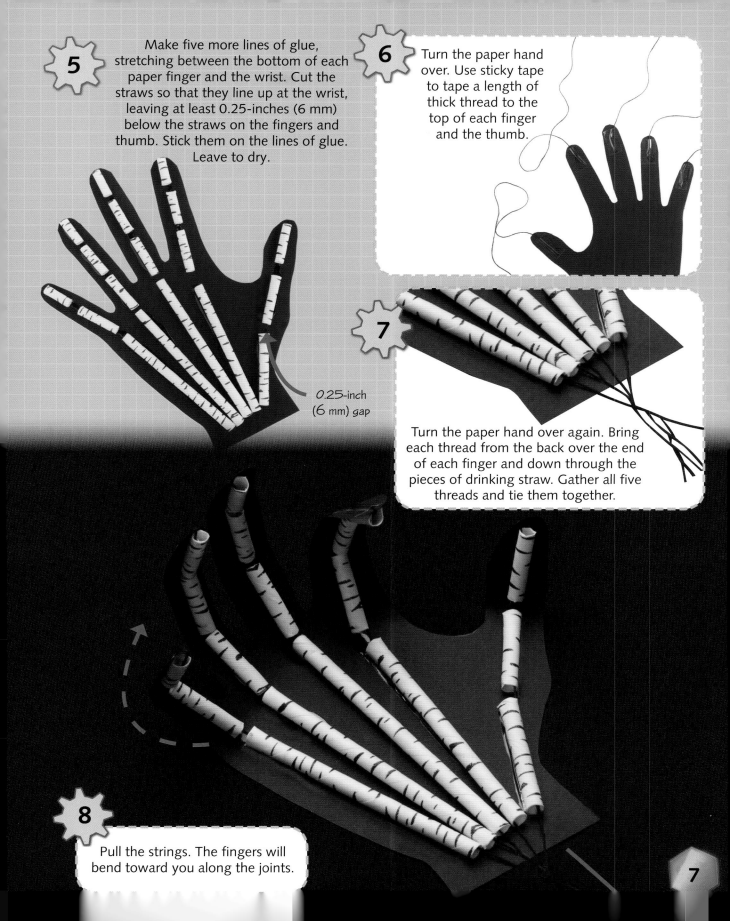

Advanced robotic hand

Amaze your friends with this almost "human" robotic hand!

The strings in the silicone hand act like the tendons and ligaments in a human hand. The flexible silicone gives the hand weight and substance to carry out simple tasks. Simple prosthetic hands work in a similar way. In real life, users often have to make choices between how well the prosthetic hand works—and how realistic it looks.

To make an advanced robotic hand, you will need:

- letter-sized sheet of thin craft foam
- pen
- silicone bath sealant gun and tube of sealant (available at most hardware stores)
- 2 pairs of disposable gloves
- 5 lengths of string, 19.5 inches (50 cm) long
- ruler • craft knife • scissors
- 5 flexible drinking straws

SAFETY FIRST
Adult participation and supervision is required for this activity. Open windows and doors before you use the silicone gun, so that no one breathes in any fumes.

1

Place your hand on the sheet of craft foam, spreading your fingers wide. Use a pen to draw around your hand.

3

Put on a pair of disposable gloves. Take one length of string and carefully lie it along a line of silicone sealant, leaving 6 inches (15 cm) below the wrist. Repeat with the other four pieces of string.

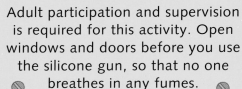

2

Ask an adult to follow the instructions to put the silicone tube into the silicone bath sealant gun and cut off the end of the nozzle. They must put on disposable gloves and draw a line of silicone from the tip of each finger to the wrist on the foam.

SAFETY FIRST
An adult must handle the silicone sealant gun.

4

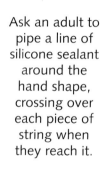

Ask an adult to pipe a line of silicone sealant around the hand shape, crossing over each piece of string when they reach it.

5

Ask an adult to fill in the shape with more silicone sealant. Use the craft knife to smooth out the sealant to make sure it completely covers the whole hand and all the strings. Leave to dry for 24 hours.

Warning!
Silicone sealant takes a long time to dry, so do not rush this stage.

6

Cut out the foam hand, taking care not to cut the strings.

7

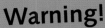

Turn the hand over so the colored foam side faces up.

9

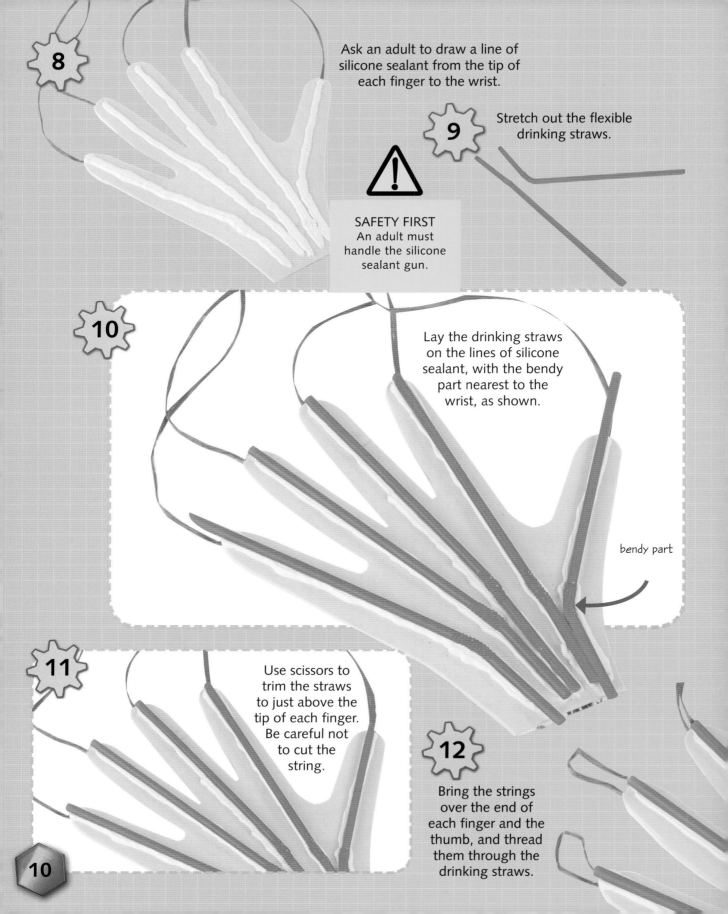

8 Ask an adult to draw a line of silicone sealant from the tip of each finger to the wrist.

9 Stretch out the flexible drinking straws.

⚠️ SAFETY FIRST
An adult must handle the silicone sealant gun.

10 Lay the drinking straws on the lines of silicone sealant, with the bendy part nearest to the wrist, as shown.

bendy part

11 Use scissors to trim the straws to just above the tip of each finger. Be careful not to cut the string.

12 Bring the strings over the end of each finger and the thumb, and thread them through the drinking straws.

13 Ask an adult to cover the hand in silicone sealant, taking care to leave each end of the drinking straws free of silicone.

SAFETY FIRST
An adult must handle the silicone sealant gun.

14 Use the craft knife to smooth out the silicone sealant. Leave until completely dry.

15 Ask an adult to help. Cut small V-shaped notches at the points shown in the photo. Cut through the silicone and the top layer of the drinking straw, but don't cut the string. This will help the fingers to bend.

16

17 Pull the strings to make the silicone hand perform simple tasks, such as gripping a ball.

Glitch Fix!

Glitch: a string was cut by mistake in steps 15/16.

Fix: pull the end back through the straw. Use a knot to re-attach it and thread it back through the drinking straw.

Bristlebot

These fun little robots skitter around at top speed.

A bristlebot is a small robot made from a toothbrush head and a vibrating motor. How does it move? As the bristlebot's motor vibrates, the vibrations make the bristles on the toothbrush head move, which makes the bristlebot "walk."

To make a bristlebot, you will need:
- battery-powered electric toothbrush (ask permission before you use it for this project)
- pliers
- wire cutter
- wire strippers
- double-sided sticky tab (available from craft stores)
- 1.5 volt button cell battery

1

Carefully use the wire cutter to snip the head off an electric toothbrush.

Pull off the bottom section of the handle.

2

Use pliers to pull out the insides of the toothbrush. (You will have to pull hard.) Remove the battery—it can be used to power something else.

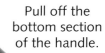

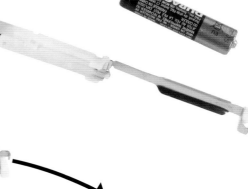

pull

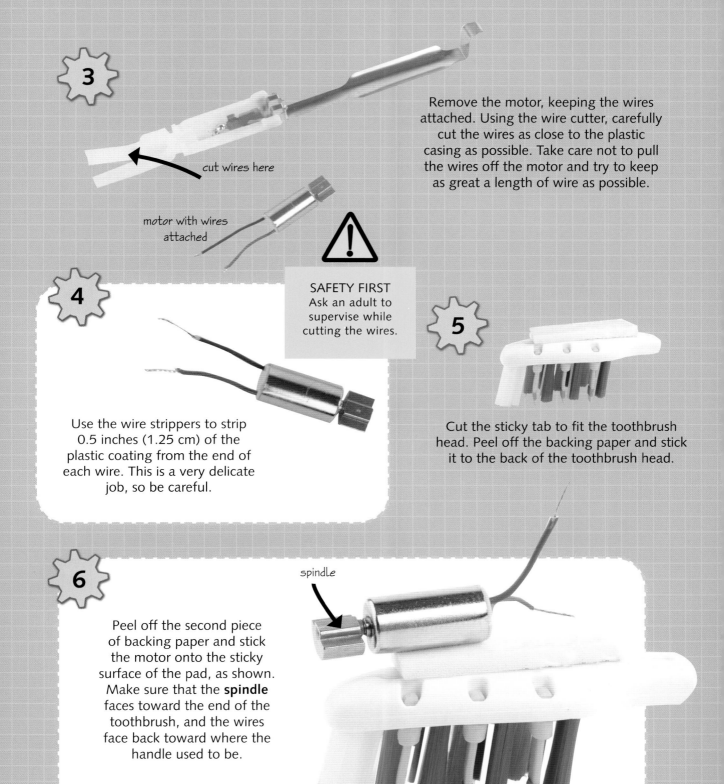

3

cut wires here

motor with wires attached

Remove the motor, keeping the wires attached. Using the wire cutter, carefully cut the wires as close to the plastic casing as possible. Take care not to pull the wires off the motor and try to keep as great a length of wire as possible.

SAFETY FIRST
Ask an adult to supervise while cutting the wires.

4

Use the wire strippers to strip 0.5 inches (1.25 cm) of the plastic coating from the end of each wire. This is a very delicate job, so be careful.

5

Cut the sticky tab to fit the toothbrush head. Peel off the backing paper and stick it to the back of the toothbrush head.

6

Peel off the second piece of backing paper and stick the motor onto the sticky surface of the pad, as shown. Make sure that the **spindle** faces toward the end of the toothbrush, and the wires face back toward where the handle used to be.

spindle

7 Press the red wire onto the sticky tab. Attach a battery on top, with the positive terminal facing down so that the bare red wire comes into contact with that positive terminal. Connect the blue (or black) wire to the top (negative terminal) by bending it onto the battery. Watch your bristlebot go!

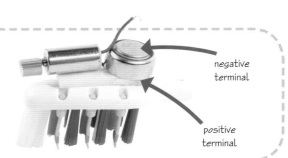

negative terminal

positive terminal

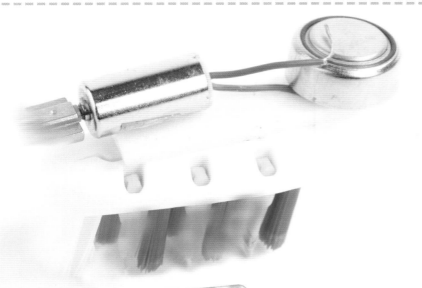

Glitch Fix!

Glitch: bristlebot is not moving very fast.

Fix: place a heavy object on the bristles of the toothbrush head to make the bristles spread out. You'll need to leave it for a few hours.

A fair test

Try racing two bristlebots over a measured distance to see which one goes farthest, fastest, and straightest.

To see if you can improve the performance of the winning bristlebot, make a second one that is identical except for one change (see right for suggestions). Race them again and record the results.

If the change you made does not improve the performance of the bristlebot, or makes it worse, change it back and think of another change that might work better. This way you can make your bristlebot into a champion.

Try racing the bristlebots on different surfaces.

Power source: you could swap this for the motor from an old mobile phone. Ask permission before you use it.

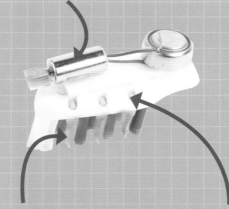

Bristles: try bending the bristles farther back.

Body: try using different toothbrush heads (they do not need to be from an electric toothbrush). You could use one with straight bristles and one with slanted bristles.

14

How to design a robot

Teams of designers focus on the coding, the sensors, and the mechanical parts of each new robot design.

tactile sensor

cameras

motion tracking sensor

distance sensors

1. The robot brain

The "brain" of a robot is run by a computer program using computer codes. The codes give all the instructions the robot needs to function. Robots are being developed with new programming (coding) systems that give the robot the ability to figure out the best way to tackle a problem. The simple robots in this book do not have any coding.

2. Robot sensors

Robots need to have sensors to tell them about their surroundings. The system of sensors delivers information to the robot brain to allow the robot to do the tasks it was built for. Robots use information about the space between objects, their size, and their shape to help them interact with their environment. There are a huge variety of sensors, from ones that detect light, sound, and movement, to those that tell the robot the temperature, distance, or pressure.

3. Robot body

The "body" of the robot is the mechanical parts that make it able to grab, turn, lift, and move. These are usually powered by air, water, electricity, or solar power. In this book, you can make robots that grab, move, turn, and even draw.

Scrub bot

Make a robot that loves to scrub!

How does a scrub bot work? The spindle on the scrub bot's motor is weighted down with a slice of cork to make it vibrate. As the motor vibrates, the vibrations cause the bristles on the nailbrush to vibrate as well, which makes the scrub bot move!

To make a scrub bot, you will need:

- 1.5v DC motor (available from electronics supplies – see p. 32)
- battery connector
- nailbrush • electrical tape
- slice of wine cork or old eraser, about 0.25 inches (6 mm) thick
- drawing compass • ruler
- 2 AA batteries
- AA battery holder
- glue • pipe cleaner
- 2 googly eyes

1

Slide the bare wire sticking out from the red plastic on the battery connector through the metal connector on the motor. Twist it back on itself to keep it in place. Repeat with the other bare wire sticking out from the black plastic-coated wire.

spindle

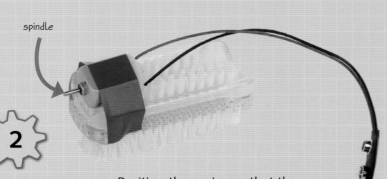

2

Position the motor so that the spindle is clear of the end of the nailbrush. Tape it in place using electrical tape.

3

Make a small hole near the edge of the piece of cork (or eraser) with the point of a compass. Keep this hole as small as possible because it needs to be a tight fit for the motor spindle.

4

connector end

Slot two AA batteries into the battery holder. Place the battery holder on top of the nailbrush, with the connector end facing the opposite way to the spindle. Use electrical tape to secure it in place.

5

Push the cork (or eraser) onto the spindle. If it is loose, take it off and put a small blob of glue into the hole. Replace the cork. Leave to set.

connectors

6

Curl the ends of the pipe cleaner around, as shown. Glue a googly eye onto each curled-up end, and glue the eye piece onto the top of the scrub bot.

7

Put your scrub bot on a flat surface and push the connector onto the battery holder. Add some dish soap and water, and set your robot to work!

Glitch Fix!

Glitch: the scrub bot is going backward.
Fix: remove the wires from the motor (step 1) and replace them the other way round.

Drawing robot

Create crazy patterns with this drawing robot!

How does it work? It uses the vibrations of the motor to make the pens wobble. They draw colorful lines on the paper as the drawing robot moves across the page.

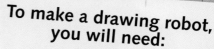
1 Use a pencil to draw around the top of the disposable cup onto the card. Cut out the card circle.

2 Hot glue the card circle onto the base of the cup.

⚠️ SAFETY FIRST
Ask an adult to supervise when you use the hot glue gun.

3 Use the tip of the compass to punch a hole through the center of the card circle and the base of the cup.

4

battery box cover

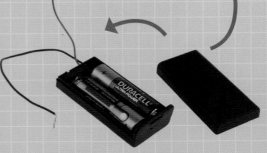

Slot two AA batteries into the battery holder. Replace the battery box cover.

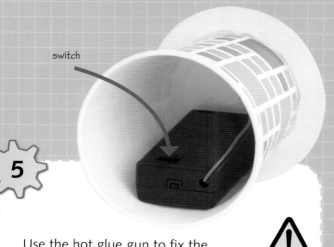

switch

5

Use the hot glue gun to fix the battery box inside the cup. The switch needs to be facing up, close to the opening of the cup.

⚠️

6

Push the black and red wires from the battery box through the holes in the base of the cup and the card circle.

Attach the red and black wires to the terminals on the motor to complete the electric circuit. Turn the battery pack on briefly to test that the motor is working.

8

7

spindle

Position the motor so that its spindle sticks out over the edge of the card circle opposite the battery box. Use the hot glue gun to fix it in place.

10

Use the hot glue gun to fix the large paper clip to the front of the cork, as shown. Leave to set.

9

⚠️

Take the slice of cork and use the compass to make a hole about 0.25 inches (6 mm) from the edge. Push it onto the spindle. It must be a tight fit. If it is loose, take it off and put a small blob of hot glue into the hole. Replace the cork. Leave to set.

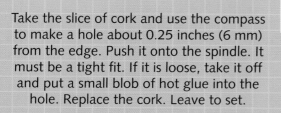

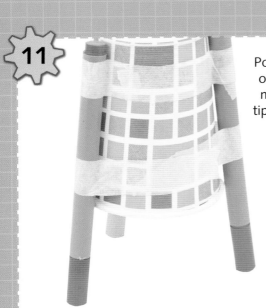

11

Position the three felt-tip pens around the outside of the cup and secure them with masking tape. Take the lids off. The pen tips now act as feet for the drawing robot.

12

Place the drawing robot onto a sheet of blank paper. Switch it on and watch the robot draw.

Glitch Fix!

Glitch: if the cup tips over, this could be for two reasons. 1) The weight of the battery pack and the motor may not be balanced. **Fix:** see which way the cup is tipping. If it is tipping toward the motor, tape a weight inside the cup opposite the motor. If it is tipping toward the battery pack, tape a weight opposite the battery pack.
2) The pens are not an equal length. **Fix:** take off the masking tape and move the pens so that the cup is evenly balanced.

Try this!

Use fabric marker pens if you want your robot to make a pattern on a piece of fabric.

Desktop robot

This desktop robot uses the power of the sun to cool you down!

Many **service robots** perform useful tasks for humans, such as mowing the lawn. How will this robot cool you down? A solar panel, which is coated in a special material, absorbs sunlight and converts it into electrical energy. The energy travels down the wires to drive the motor that is attached to the propeller. The propeller whizzes around, creating a cooling flow of air.

To make a desktop robot, you will need:
- sheet of stiff card stock, 12.2 inches x 4 inches (31 cm x 10 cm)
- sheet of colored wrapping paper, 12.2 inches x 4 inches (31 cm x 10 cm)
- ruler • pencil
- glue and spreader
- craft knife
- micro motor (4v solar micro motor 47,000 rpm), propeller, and solar panel kit (available from most electronics stores)
- small screwdriver

1 Cover one side of the card stock with glue. Attach to the wrapping paper. Leave to dry.

2 Turn the card over. Use the ruler and pencil to make marks 4 inches (10 cm) apart. Fold the card along the edge of the ruler at each mark and along the 0.5 inches (1 cm) tab mark at the end.

0.5 inches (I cm)

4 inches (10 cm)   4 inches (10 cm)   4 inches (10 cm)

3 Use the ruler and pencil to draw diagonal lines across each 4 inch (10 cm) square section of card.

21

4 Place the motor where the lines cross on the end section without the tab. Draw around the motor. Ask an adult to help you cut out the card circle using a craft knife.

5 Make a small hole in the center of the middle section of the card using the point of the screwdriver.

⚠️ **SAFETY FIRST**
Ask an adult to supervise while using the screwdriver.

6 Turn the card over. Push the motor into place in the hole you made in step 4. Make sure the spindle faces out on the patterned side, and add the propeller.

7 Push the wires connected to the solar panel through the small hole in the middle section of the card.

8 Glue the solar panel in place in the center of the middle panel.

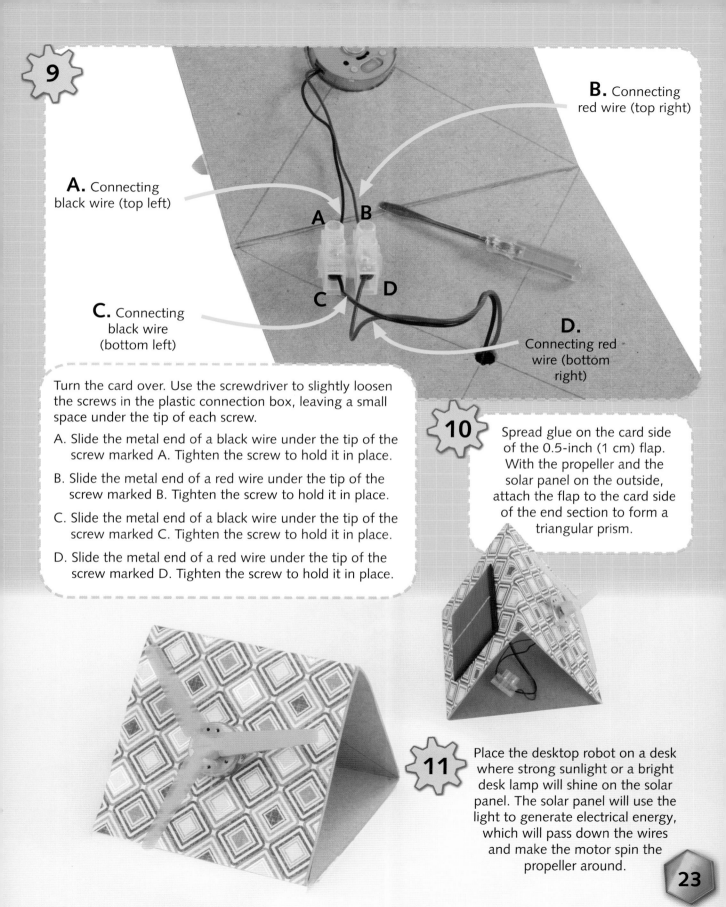

9

A. Connecting black wire (top left)

B. Connecting red wire (top right)

C. Connecting black wire (bottom left)

D. Connecting red wire (bottom right)

Turn the card over. Use the screwdriver to slightly loosen the screws in the plastic connection box, leaving a small space under the tip of each screw.

A. Slide the metal end of a black wire under the tip of the screw marked A. Tighten the screw to hold it in place.

B. Slide the metal end of a red wire under the tip of the screw marked B. Tighten the screw to hold it in place.

C. Slide the metal end of a black wire under the tip of the screw marked C. Tighten the screw to hold it in place.

D. Slide the metal end of a red wire under the tip of the screw marked D. Tighten the screw to hold it in place.

10 Spread glue on the card side of the 0.5-inch (1 cm) flap. With the propeller and the solar panel on the outside, attach the flap to the card side of the end section to form a triangular prism.

11 Place the desktop robot on a desk where strong sunlight or a bright desk lamp will shine on the solar panel. The solar panel will use the light to generate electrical energy, which will pass down the wires and make the motor spin the propeller around.

Robbo the robot

Build your own Robbo the robot!

The gear box kit includes an electric motor powered by batteries. This is attached to a metal **axle**, which has wheels attached to it. When you turn the motor on, it turns the back axle of Robbo, making it move forward. The axle is attached to the arms which turn as the wheels move.

To make Robbo the robot, you will need:

- ruler • pen
- potato chip tube with lid
- measuring tape
- marker pen
- screwdriver • scissors
- silver spray paint
- drinking straw, cut to 4 inches (10 cm) long
- 3v worm drive gear box kit (available from most electronics stores)
- hot glue gun
- 2 elastic band
- 2 wooden skewer, 4.7 inches (12 cm) long
- 4 plastic caps (from small plastic drink bottles)
- wooden craft stick (available from craft stores)
- polystyrene ball, 3 inch (8 cm) diameter
- polystyrene ball, 0.5 inch (1.25 cm) diameter

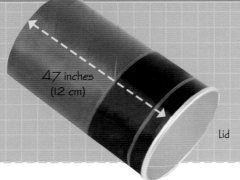

4.7 inches (12 cm)

lid

1 Use the ruler and pen to mark a line around the potato chip tube, 4.7 inches (12 cm) from the top with lid. Ask an adult to cut along this line. Discard the bottom tube piece.

SAFETY FIRST
Ask an adult to supervise while using the screwdriver.

2 0.5 inches (1 cm)

draw a line

Wrap the measuring tape around the cut edge of the tube, 0.5 inches (1.25 cm) from the edge. Draw a line above the edge of the measuring tape.

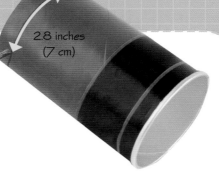

2.8 inches (7 cm)

3 Make two marks 2.8 inches (7 cm) apart along the line. Use the screwdriver to make a hole at each mark.

4

Enlarge the holes by pushing the end of a pen into them and twisting it. They need to be just large enough for a drinking straw to slide through.

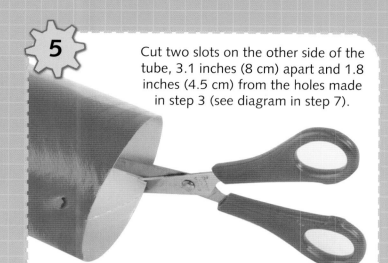

5

Cut two slots on the other side of the tube, 3.1 inches (8 cm) apart and 1.8 inches (4.5 cm) from the holes made in step 3 (see diagram in step 7).

6

Make a hole at the top of each slit with the screwdriver. They need to be large enough for the axles attached to the gear box to rotate freely (see page 26).

7

The tube should look like this from the top.

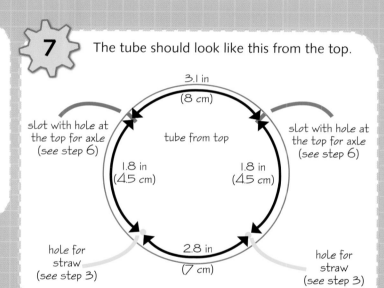

3.1 in
(8 cm)

slot with hole at the top for axle
(see step 6)

tube from top

slot with hole at the top for axle
(see step 6)

1.8 in
(4.5 cm)

1.8 in
(4.5 cm)

hole for straw
(see step 3)

2.8 in
(7 cm)

hole for straw
(see step 3)

8

Spray the tube with silver paint. Leave to dry.

⚠️

SAFETY FIRST
Ask an adult to supervise when you use the spray paint. Be sure to open a window to make sure you don't breathe in any fumes.

9

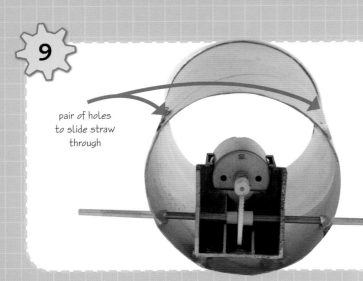

pair of holes to slide straw through

Slide the axle into the two slots and into the holes you made in steps 5–6. Use the hot glue gun to glue the plastic part of the motor inside the tube. Leave to dry.

Slide the drinking straw through the top pair of holes you made in steps 3–4.

SAFETY FIRST
Ask an adult to supervise when you use the hot glue gun.

10

Turn the model around. Attach the wires from the battery pack to the motor. Hot glue the battery pack to the inside of the tube, with the switch near to the uncut edge of the tube.

11

Slide one side of the axle out of the slot. Slide an elastic band over the end of the axle. Push the axle back into through the slot so that the elastic band is between the motor and the slot. Repeat with the other side of the axle.

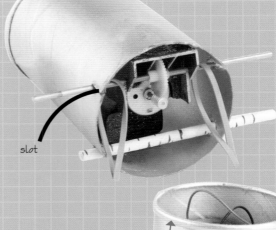

slot

12

Use the ruler to make a mark, 1.6 inches (4 cm) from the top edge, and in between the axle and the drinking straw. Use the screwdriver to make a hole at this point. Repeat on the opposite side of the tube.

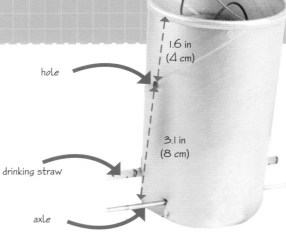

hole

1.6 in (4 cm)

3.1 in (8 cm)

drinking straw

axle

13

Feed the elastic bands up to the top of the tube, near what will become the arm holes. Slide a wooden skewer through the hole in the tube you created in step 12, through both the elastic bands and through the hole opposite.

14

Ask an adult to poke a hole through the center of each bottle cap. The hole must be big enough for one of the wooden skewers to fit through.

15

Spray the bottle caps with silver paint.

16

Slide a wooden skewer through the drinking straw. Push a bottle cap onto each end to give Robbo wheels. Leave about 0.25 inches (6 mm) of skewer sticking out. Repeat to add wheels to the other axle.

17

Use scissors to cut the wooden craft stick in half. Make a small hole in the middle of one end with a screwdriver, 0.5 inches (1.25 cm) from the top edge. Repeat with the other half. Spray the craft sticks silver. Leave to dry.

18

hot glue

Push the craft sticks onto the ends of the wooden skewer you attached in step 13 to make arms for Robbo. If the skewer is not a tight fit, glue it in place with the hot glue gun.

SAFETY FIRST
Ask an adult to supervise when you use the hot glue gun.

19

Ask an adult to cut the large polystyrene ball in half. Use the hot glue gun to stick one half onto the lid of the potato chip tube.

Hot glue the small polystyrene ball onto the large polystyrene ball. Spray the whole thing with silver paint. Leave to dry.

Glitch Fix!
Glitch: the arms do not move.
Fix: the elastic band is too loose or too tight. Try different sizes of elastic band until you find one that works.

20

Push the lid in place to give Robbo a head. Place Robbo on a flat surface. Turn on the motor and off he whizzes!

Try this!
Decorate Robbo with paint or stickers. Add details such as hair, hands, and eyes.

Milestones in the history of robots

Greek philosopher and mathematician Archytas of Tarentum built a wooden bird that could flap its wings.

400 BCE

1495

Leonardo da Vinci drew plans for a humanoid robot that could move its head and sit up.

1700–1900

Automatons, mechanical puppets of animals or figures, became popular. The most famous of them was a mechanical duck, designed by Jacques de Vaucanson, which could stretch its neck, flap its wings, and swallow and digest food.

British mathematician Charles Babbage started work on his Analytical Machine, one of the first computational machines.

1833

The word "robot" was first used in a play by Czech writer Karel Capek. In the play, an inventor creates human-like machines, called robots, and the people in the play are killed or enslaved by them.

1921

1932

The first robot toy called Lilliput was produced in Japan. It was a tin wind-up toy that could walk.

American writer Isaac Asimov introduced the three laws of robotics in his story *Runaround*.

1942

1943

British mathematician Alan Turing devised a test to see if a computer can really think for itself. This test has become known as the "Turing Test."

1950

The world's first electronic computer, Colossus, was built in Britain to crack Nazi coded messages.

The Stanford Cart was one of the first mobile robots controlled by computers. It was able to navigate across a room full of chairs.

1961

The first industrial robot was used on the assembly line at General Motors in the United States to make cars.

American engineer Victor Scheinman developed a programmable robot arm, which became widely used in factories.

1975

1981

Canadarm, a remotely operated robotic "arm," performed its first tasks in space.

NASA's Sojourner robot rover carried out a series of science experiments on Mars.

1997

2000

The United Nations estimated that there were 742,500 industrial robots in use worldwide.

The tiny da Vinci robot was first used in heart surgery in Canada to unblock a patient's arteries.

2007

2002

The Roomba robotic vacuum cleaner was sold in large numbers.

Robots are an important part of our everyday lives.

Today

Template

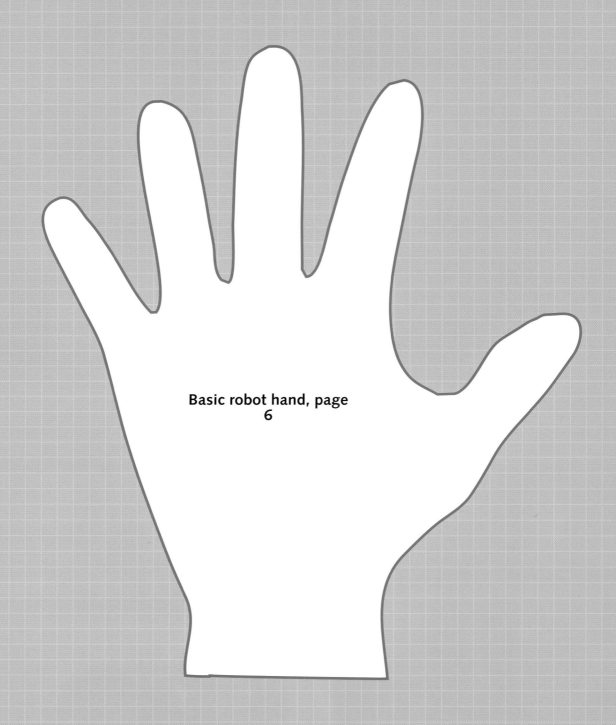

Basic robot hand, page 6

Glossary

autonomous To act independently or have the freedom to do so

axle A rod or spindle that passes through the center of a wheel

blood vessels Tubes (veins, arteries, and capillaries) that carry blood around the body

contaminated An object or area that has been poisoned or made hazardous in some way

ligament A short band of tough, fibrous material that connects two bones together

mechanical The working parts of a machine

myoelectric Using electric signals naturally made by muscles to control an artifical limb

prosthesis An artificial limb

radiation A type of dangerous energy that is produced by radioactive substances

sensor A device that detects or measures things

service robot A robot that performs useful tasks for humans

spindle The rotating small metal rod attached to an electric motor

tendon A tough flexible cord of fibrous material that attaches a muscle to a bone

Learning More

Books
Amstutz, Lisa J. *All About Robots*. Focus Readers, 2017.
Otfinoski, Steven. *Making Robots: Science, Technology, and Engineering*. Children's Press, 2016.
Sjonger, Rebecca. *Robotics Engineering and Our Automated World*. Crabtree Publishing, 2017.

Websites
Discover how to make your own Mars rover here:
www.nasa.gov/sites/default/files/atoms/files/mars_survival_kit_-_rover_final_4.pdf

Learn how to drive a Mars rover without draining all of its battery power:
www.nasa.gov/audience/foreducators/robotics/home/ROVER.html#.VmbUA7TJt0I

Watch a video of a really cool robot here:
www.wimp.com/coolestrobot/

Index